BIOLOGY Field Notes

Be a NAKED MOLE RAT Expert

by
Alex Hall

BEARPORT
PUBLISHING

Minneapolis, Minnesota

Credits

All images are courtesy of Shutterstock.com, unless otherwise specified. With thanks to Alamy, Getty Images, Thinkstock Photo, and iStockphoto.

Recurring – yana shypova, vectorplus, NotionPic, Diqdaya, The_Pixel, Milano M, Macrovector, AstarteJulia, DreamStockIcons, Kostenyukova Nataliya. Character throughout – NotionPic. Cover – Eric Isselee, Ricardo J de E, Milano M, Macrovector, AstarteJulia, DreamStockIcons, Kostenyukova Nataliya. 4–5 – Neil Bromhall, Aydan Metev. 6–7 – Aydan Metev, Neil Bromhall, GlobalP. 8–9 – Aydan Metev, Neil Bromhall, GlobalP. 10–11 – KenKris, Neil Bromhall, blickwinkel, christopher babcock. 12–13 – belizar, Neil Bromhall. 14–15 – Neil Bromhall. 16–17 – Neil Bromhall, Paul Lloyd, reptiles4all. 18–19 – Danny Ye, Neil Bromhall. 20–21 – Neil Bromhall, Aydan Metev. 22–23 – belizar, Aydan Metev.

Bearport Publishing Company Product Development Team

Publisher: Jen Jenson; Director of Product Development: Spencer Brinker; Managing Editor: Allison Juda; Editor: Cole Nelson; Associate Editor: Naomi Reich; Associate Editor: Tiana Tran; Designer: Kim Jones; Designer: Kayla Eggert; Designer: Steve Scheluchin; Production Specialist: Owen Hamlin

Library of Congress Cataloging-in-Publication Data is available at www.loc.gov or upon request from the publisher.

ISBN: 979-8-89577-007-8 (hardcover)
ISBN: 979-8-89577-438-0 (paperback)
ISBN: 979-8-89577-124-2 (ebook)

© 2026 BookLife Publishing
This edition is published by arrangement with BookLife Publishing.

North American adaptations © 2026 Bearport Publishing Company. All rights reserved. No part of this publication may be reproduced in whole or in part, stored in any retrieval system, or transmitted in any form or by any means, electronic, mechanical, photocopying, recording, or otherwise, without written permission from the publisher. Bearport Publishing is a division of FlutterBee Education Group.

For more information, write to Bearport Publishing, 5357 Penn Avenue South, Minneapolis, MN 55419.

CONTENTS

Meet the Biologist............4

A Naked Mole Rat's Body......6

Underground Homes.........10

The Colony.................12

Family Life.................14

Dinner Time................16

Pooping Time...............18

Life Cycle.................20

Noisy Naked Mole Rats.......22

Glossary..................24

Index....................24

A NAKED MOLE RAT'S BODY

Many **mammals** have fur that protects their skin from the sun. But not naked mole rats! These rodents spend their lives underground, so they need very little hair. However, the rats do have about 100 thin whiskers that help them feel the world around them.

Whiskers

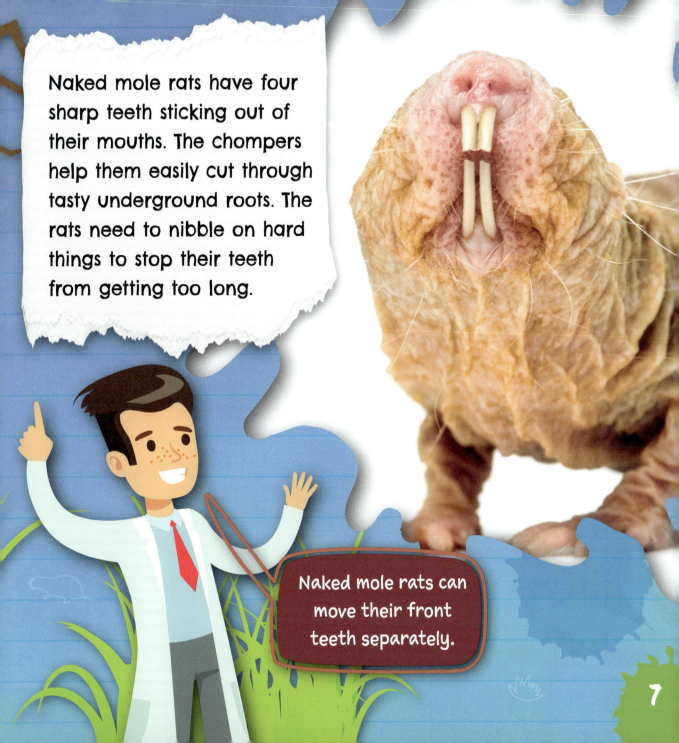

Naked mole rats have four sharp teeth sticking out of their mouths. The chompers help them easily cut through tasty underground roots. The rats need to nibble on hard things to stop their teeth from getting too long.

Naked mole rats can move their front teeth separately.

Naked mole rats are very small. Most of them are around 3 inches (8 cm) long and weigh only 1 ounce (28 g). These rodents have short legs, which lets them run just as easily backward as they can forward.

Naked mole rats get their name from their hairless-looking bodies.

These rodents have tiny eyes, so they do not see well in their underground homes. But the rats have good senses of touch and smell. They use these senses to get around and learn about the world.

Naked mole rats close their eyes when running through tunnels.

UNDERGROUND HOMES

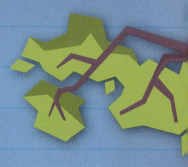

Naked mole rats are found in East Africa. The wrinkly animals live in underground habitats called **burrows**. These mazelike holes have many rooms. Each room is used for something different, such as eating, pooping, or looking after young.

A habitat is the place where a plant or animal lives.

Some naked mole rat burrows are almost 3 miles (5 km) long!

Naked mole rats live in large groups called colonies. Colonies can have anywhere from 20 to 300 rats. Every group has a queen, who is the colony's leader.

THE COLONY

Aside from the queen, there are two other kinds of naked mole rats in a colony.

Only two kinds of rodents have queens. They are naked mole rats and Damaraland mole rats.

A soldier rat

Soldier rats keep the colony safe from **predators**. When facing an enemy, these rats pile on top of one another and show their teeth.

Worker rats dig tunnels and search for food. They also look out for predators. If a predator enters their burrow, the worker rats let out an alarm call to warn the soldiers.

A worker rat

Most of the naked mole rats in a colony are workers.

FAMILY LIFE

Naked mole rats **communicate** with one another in many different ways. These social animals can hiss, grunt, or chirp. Each rat colony has its own soft chirp to help its members recognize others from the group.

Naked mole rats cannot keep their bodies warm.

At night, it can get pretty cold in naked mole rat tunnels. How do the rats keep warm? They huddle together while sleeping!

DINNER TIME

When it's time to eat, naked mole rats find food by searching their burrows. These rodents are herbivores. That means they eat plants, such as roots.

Naked mole rat teeth are so strong they can chew through concrete.

Naked mole rats get all the water they need from their food. But the rats also have to avoid becoming food. Snakes are the main predators of these rodents.

A rufous beaked snake

A Kenyan sand boa

POOPING TIME

Roots are not the only things that naked mole rats eat. They also snack on their own poop! Chowing down on poopy leftovers helps the rats get more **nutrients** from their food.

Naked mole rats save time and energy by eating their poop instead of digging for more food.

Poop also helps naked mole rats keep track of their colony. They do this by rolling around in their shared poop room. If a naked mole rat smells different, then that means it is from another group.

Pee-yew! Good thing these animals stay underground.

LIFE CYCLE

In a colony, the queen is the only one who gives birth. She can have up to 28 baby rats, or pups. The queen may have babies as often as 5 times a year! As the rodents grow, they can live for around 30 years.

A life cycle includes the different stages of an animal's life.

Being the queen is not for the weak. The **female** naked mole rats in a colony must fight to become queen and then fight off other females to stay in charge. When a queen dies, the other females will battle to determine who is strong enough to take over.

Sometimes, female naked mole rats fight each other to the death!

NOISY NAKED MOLE RATS

From chirping to hissing, naked mole rats are noisy! I hope you've enjoyed learning about these amazing rodents.

GLOSSARY

biologist a person who studies and knows a lot about living things

burrows holes or tunnels in the ground made by an animal to live in

communicate to share information

expert a person who knows a lot about something

female a naked mole rat that can give birth

mammals animals that are warm-blooded, drink milk from their mothers when they are young, and have fur

nutrients things that are found in food and that are needed to stay healthy

predators animals that hunt other animals for food

rodents small mammals with long front teeth, such as mice, rats, rabbits, and beavers

INDEX

eyes 9
hairs 6, 8
plants 10, 16
predators 12–13, 17

queens 11–12, 20–21
skin 6, 8
snakes 17
soldiers 12–13

teeth 7, 12, 16
tunnels 9, 13, 15
water 17
workers 13